TO BE OR NOT TO BE A CHURCH MEMBER?, THAT IS THE QUESTION!

TO BE

or

NOT TO BE

A CHURCH MEMBER?,
that IS THE QUESTION!

WAYNE MACK

Foreword by Daniel Kirk

CALVARY PRESS PUBLISHING

Calvary Press Publishing

ISBN 1-879737-57-4

1. Church Life   2. Christian Life   3. Ministry
4. Christian Counseling   5. Applied Theology

Cover and Book Design: Anthony Rotolo

Manufactured in the USA
1 2 3 4 5 6 7 8 9 10   04 05 06 07 08

CONTENTS

There is nothing outside the Trinity itself that God loves more than the church for which He died. Sadly, many Christians don't share Christ's degree of affection and devotion for His bride, and often are ashamed to identify themselves with her. This is perhaps nowhere more evident than in the general indifference toward formal membership in a local church.

Dr. Mack is exactly right when he asserts "many Christians in our day think no more highly of membership in the church than membership in a local country club." Unfortunately, I believe his finger is right on the pulse of western Christianity. We tend to align ourselves with all the wrong things. We're all too happy to identify with a favorite recreation, business institution or political movement. Many of us are even eager to wear t-shirts and jackets that boldly proclaim our unapologetic allegiance to our favorite sports teams. But what about identifying ourselves with the one thing in the created universe that God loves supremely? Where is our bold and unapologetic display of allegiance to the church?

Thankfully, many precious saints recognize intuitively their need to formally commit themselves to a local body of believers. They're eager to help the pastors of their church lead "with joy and not with grief" (Hebrews 13:17). They understand that a lack of formal commitment would make their relationship to their spiritual leaders ambiguously undefined. They take seriously the warning of Jesus that "whoever is ashamed of Me and My words in this adulterous and sinful generation, the Son of Man will also be ashamed of him when He comes in the glory of His Father with the holy angels" (Mark 8:38). All too often, however, this is not the case.

I believe one of the greatest needs in the western church of the twenty-first century is a return to a decisive commitment to the Lord Jesus Christ made powerfully tangible by commitment to the local church. Building His church is the only thing Christ is doing in the world; so committing to a local body that is passionate about living for Christ must be the highest privilege in the world. Where else can a believer know more joy in employing his spiritual gifts than in the local church? What other institution can better encourage the believer's pursuit of holiness with real accountability (Matthew 18) than the local church? To what other organization did God specifically give such gifted men as pastor/teachers (Ephesians 4) than the church? To what spiritual leaders are disciples of the risen Christ commanded to obey other than those of the local church? Can a follower of Jesus Christ profess allegiance to Him and deny the church for which He died?

The book you hold in your hand tackles all of these issues and more in an attempt to encourage each of us who name the name of Christ to consider our commitment to the local church. I'm confident you will come away convinced that membership in a local body of believers is biblically imperative. Every believer should wrestle with this issue. Every Pastor should address it. This book can help.

Pastor Daniel Kirk
Calvary Bible Church
Fort Worth, TX

THE QUESTION

Professing Christians in the twenty first century are asking amazing questions about the church and coming up with different answers. The questions: Should I join a church or not join a church? Is church membership an essential or optional matter for Christians? Is it the main option for Christian growth and service or one of many options? Is church membership important or unimportant? Is it a matter of obedience to the Lord or a matter of choice for the individual Christian?

What about you? What are your convictions about church membership? Are you for it or against it? Is it fine for some, but not necessary for others? How would you answer these questions and why would you answer them the way you do? And, if you do have an answer to these questions, what is your authority for answering as you do? Is it your own opinion, the opinions of others—or the Bible?

In this book I will begin by describing how some in our time have answered this question. I will present the traditional view and, finally, give you what I'm convinced is God's perspective on the issue raised by these questions.

Church Membership: A "Modern" View

In our day, there are many professing Christians who believe that church membership is an option. If asked, they would say that it's not important, and certainly not a requirement, for believers to identify with a local church in a formal way. To them, joining or not joining a church is something like deciding which version of the Bible to use, or deciding whether or not to vote in an election; or deciding whether to eat meat or be a vegetarian. In the same way, these people would say that church membership is simply a matter of preference.

In my over forty years of ministry, I've had many people say to me, "I'm not saved by church membership; I'm saved by the grace of God through faith. When I get to heaven, I'm not going to be there because I joined a church, but because I repented of my sins and believed on Jesus Christ. So what difference does it make whether I'm a member of a local church or not? After all, I can be just as good a Christian without being a church member as I can by being one. In fact, I know lots of people who are members of a church and they're hypocrites. Their lives are certainly no better than mine. Membership is optional."

In his book, *Exit Interviews,* William Hendricks indicates that he does not believe that church membership or involvement is essential for believers. He notes in his book that, in recent years, there has been a surge in church attendance, but he says:

There's a dark side to recent reports of church

attendance in North America. While countless unchurched people may be flocking in the
front door of the church, a steady stream of the
church is flowing quietly out the back. It's esti-
mated that 53,000 people leave churches every
week and never come back.[1]

He goes on to describe numerous interviews that
he has had with people who had left the church
and which led him to the conclusion that there are
numerous, valid options for a believer's spiritual
growth apart from the local church. He wrote:

> Despite glowing reports of attendance, more
> and more Christians in North America are
> feeling disillusioned with the church and other
> formal institutional expressions of Christianity.
> That's not to say that these back-door believ-
> ers have given up on the faith. On the contrary,
> they may be quite articulate regarding spiritual
> matters. Indeed, some have remarkably vibrant
> spiritual lives and touchingly close friendships
> with a kindred spirit or two. But in the main,
> they tend to nurture their relationship with God
> apart from the traditional means of church at-
> tendance and church membership…God is do-
> ing His marvelous work in someone's life even
> apart from the church, believe it or not.[2]

In the final chapter, Hendricks addresses these
"dropouts" that he has interviewed in this way:

> I'm extremely reluctant to shake my finger in
> your face and say, "You turn right around and
> get yourself back into a church." I don't know

your circumstances. It may be that there are lots of alternatives around you, in which case I certainly would encourage you to explore them diligently until you find something that works. Tradition holds that you cannot grow apart from a church. How then will you proceed, assuming that you want to proceed, if you don't want to become part of a church? A few of the people I've interviewed have moved forward by standing tradition on its head and taking spiritual sustenance wherever they can find it-—from books, magazines, television radio ministries, a sympathetic friend or two, perhaps the arts and music, maybe volunteer work. Over time, they've become quite resourceful in finding ways to meet God apart from a local church…I don't blame you for walking out.[3]

Hendricks, who obviously does not believe that church membership or attendance is essential, is far from being alone in this matter. He is merely expressing what a growing number of professing Christians think and feel about the importance of involvement in the local church.

Church Membership: An Historic View

It's important for us to realize, however, that this "modern" view of church membership stands in stark contrast to the view of many prominent Christian leaders of the faith throughout church history. St. Augustine, in the fourth century, said: "He cannot have God for his Father who does not have the church for his mother." Martin Luther, after he had left the Roman Catholic priesthood, said, "Apart from the church, salvation is impossible."

Many other Christian leaders of the past had strong views on the importance of church membership. John Bunyan, the author of *The Pilgrim's Progress,* wrote a poem of 130 lines in which each one extolled the importance of the church and of believers being involved in the church. R.B. Kuiper, a Dutch theologian in the early twentieth century, wrote a book called, *The Glorious Body of Christ.* In it he wrote this about the importance of church membership:

> It's clear that in the days of the apostles, it was the universal practice to receive believers into the visible church. It's possible that a true believer, because of some unusual circumstances, may fail to unite with the church. One may, for instance, believe in Christ and die before receiving baptism, or joining a local church. But such instances are exceptional. The Scriptural rule is that while membership is not a prerequisite for salvation, it is a necessary consequence of salvation. [4]

Timothy Dwight, a well-known pastor at the beginning of the 1800's, believed that the local church was an essential part of every believer's life, from the new birth until physical death. He wrote a wonderful hymn about the church that many of us are familiar with called "I Love Thy Kingdom, Lord":

> I love Thy kingdom, Lord, the house of Thine abode,
> The church our blest Redeemer saved with His own precious blood.

I love Thy church, O God! Her walls before
Thee stand,
Dear as the apple of Thine eye, and graven on
Thy hand.
For her my tears shall fall; for her my prayers
ascend;
To her my cares and toils be giv'n, till toils and
cares shall end.
Beyond my highest joy I prize her heav'nly
ways,
Her sweet communion, solemn vows, her
hymns of love and praise.

John Calvin, one of the reformers, stated:

It's now our intention to discuss the visible
church. Let us learn even from the title "mother." There is no other way to enter into life unless
this mother conceive us in her womb, give us
birth, nourish us at her breast, and lastly, unless
she keep us under her care and guidance, until
the time when we put off mortal flesh and we
become like the angels. Our weakness does not
allow us to be dismissed from the school of the
church until we have been pupils all our lives.
Furthermore, away from her bosom, one cannot
hope for any forgiveness of sins or any salvation.
God's fatherly care and the especial witness of
spiritual life are limited to His flock.[5]

More recently, Robert Saucy, after much biblical
study and a knowledge of church history, drew this
conclusion about the importance of the church in
the life of the Christian and the program of God:

Throughout the course of history God has worked in a variety of ways through individuals, nations, and peoples. The focus of his present work is the church. That which was begun in the Scriptures, as men and women were called to acknowledge the Lordship of Christ, continues today in fulfillment of Christ's promise to build His church. Not only is Christ building His church, but also it is the primary instrument through which He ministers in the world. As the Father sent Christ, so the church bears the ambassadorial role for its Lord as sent ones with a message of reconciliation.

...the follower of Jesus Christ cannot profess allegiance to Him and deny His church. What is needed far more than denunciations is...renewed effort to seek God's ways in which one may be a part of the building process.[6]

There has been, and continues to be, much debate about the idea of the visible church versus the invisible church, or the universal church versus the local church. While the Scripture uses only one word, *ekklesia*, to mean "church," it is true that all of these variations—local, universal, visible, and invisible church—are indicated by different passages in the Word of God.

According to Scripture, the *invisible* church includes everyone who has ever been genuinely born again from every age of church history. This church will not meet in a visible way until Christ returns. The *visible* church consists of believers who are alive and meeting together right now. In a similar way, the *universal* church is not any particular local assembly, but all of God's people around the world. Finally, the local church is a regular gathering together for worship and ministry of a specific group of people in a specific area.

Many Christians believe the only thing that really matters is membership in the **invisible** or the *universal* church—the worldwide body of believers. Membership in a *local* church, on the other hand, is of little importance to them. However, when we consider what the Bible has to say about the church, it is important to distinguish when the word "church" is used to indicate the local church, and when it is used to indicate the universal, or invisible church.

The word "church" is used one hundred ten times in the New Testament, and it is instructive to note that ninety-three of those are clear references to the *local* church. More than that, in only seventeen out of a hundred ten times in which the word "church" appears to signify the universal rather than the local church, it is apparent from the context that the idea of the local church cannot be eliminated from the meaning of some of those references. We may conclude from this large number of references that the Bible has quite a lot to say about the importance of the local church.

Scripture speaks very clearly to the fact that identification with God's people in a formal, public way was considered essential in both Old Testament and New Testament times. In the Old Testament, non-Jews who wished to be part of God's covenant people were required to undergo circumcision. They were then expected to follow all the instructions for worship; sacrifice, cleanliness, and eating that were laid out for God's people in the Law. Similarly, a careful study of the New Testament doesn't reveal even a hint of any believer who was truly saved, but not part of a local church.

In reference to the idea that being a part of the universal church or what is often called the invisible church is all that really matters for the Christian, R. B. Kuiper writes:

> It is clear that in the days of the apostles it was the universal practice to receive believers into the visible church.
>
> What could be more logical? He who believes in Christ is united with Christ. Faith binds him to Christ. He is a member of Christ's body, the invisible church. But the visible church is but the outward manifestation of that body. Every member of the invisible church should, as a matter of course, be a member of the visible church. Extremely significant in this connection is Acts 2:47: "And the Lord added to the church daily such as should be saved." Not only does the Lord Christ require of those who are saved that they unite with the church; He Himself joins them to the church. And the reference is unmistakably to the visible church.
>
> …The Scriptural rule is that, while membership in the church is not a prerequisite of salvation, it is a necessary consequence of salvation.[7]

We may conclude, then, that the historic view of church membership is that it is an essential part of every true believer's Christian life. It is not enough for us to merely say that we're a part of God's universal or invisible church. Though we're a part of that church by virtue of salvation, we must also make a commitment to a specific local group of God's people.

Even more important, however, than the testimony of these historic witnesses, is the testimony of Scripture itself. The Word of God has much to teach us about the character and responsibilities of the local church. In the next several chapters of this study, we're going to look at ten biblical reasons that I believe make it absolutely clear that church membership and involvement is a requirement for every true believer in Christ.

Application/Discussion Questions

1. Summarize the perspective on church membership described in the book *Exit Interviews*.

2. What reasons have you heard people give for not becoming a member of a church?

3. What is your perspective on membership in a local church?

4. If someone were to ask you, "Why should I become a member of a local church," what would you tell him or her?

5. What is the historic view about the importance of the church in God's program? What metaphors did some of the Christian leaders of the past use in describing their perspective on the importance of the church?

6. How many times is the word church used in the New Testament?

7. What is the significance of the fact that when the Bible uses the word "church" it is usually referring to a local, visible church?

1. William Hendricks, *Exit Interviews* (Chicago: Moody Publishers, 1993), pp. 17-19
2. Ibid., pp.17-19
3. Ibid., pp.295,300
4. R.B. Kuiper, *The Glorious Body of Christ* (Grand Rapids: Eerdmans Publishing, 1996), pp. 112-113
5. John Calvin, *Institutes of the Christian Religion, translated by R.F. Battles* (Philadelphia: Westminster Press, 1996), sec. 2:1012
6. Robert Saucy, *The Church in God's Program* (Chicago: Moody Press, 1973), p.7
7. Op. cit., pp.111-112

Why is church membership an essential part of every believer's life? Why have godly men throughout history considered it to be so important that they've preached about it, written about it, and composed hymns extolling it? In the next three chapters I want to present at least ten biblical reasons for considering membership and church involvement to be an important issue for every believer.

It's important for all believers to consider these ten points for several reasons. First, if you *are* a member of a local church, it's important for you to be able to talk with those who are not and to encourage them to become members by presenting these biblical reasons for church membership. Second, if you *are not* a member of a local church, it is important for you to consider these biblical reasons so that you will change your situation and take steps to become a member. Third, every church member needs to understand the privileges that church membership opens to them as well as the commitments to which they're called by their church membership.

CHAPTER 2

Reason Number One For Church Membership:
The "One Anothering" Commands of Scripture

Every Christian ought to be a member of a local church because the breadth and depth of our biblical responsibilities to other Christians requires it. We cannot rightly fulfill our biblical responsibilities to other believers without being a part of a local church.

Many of our responsibilities to other believers are spelled out in terms of the "one another commands" found throughout Scripture. There are fifty-eight "one another commands" in the Word of God, and, realistically understood, it's impossible to understand how these commands may be truly fulfilled towards other believers without committed involvement in a local church.

John 13:34-35 contains this "one another command": "A new command I give to you, that you love one another, even as I have loved you, that you also *love one another.* By this all men will know that you are my disciples, if you *have love for one another.*" Galatians 5:13 says, "For you were called to freedom, brethren; only do not turn your freedom into an opportunity for the flesh, but through love *serve one another.*" In Romans 12:10, Paul commanded us, "*Be devoted to one another* in brotherly love; *give preference to one another in honor.*"

In these verses, the Word of God is calling us to a certain kind of life that is necessarily tied to the lives of other people. We're called to love and serve one another, and with such regularity and passion that our love and service may be described as devotion. Scripture indicates that as believers we have been set apart for loving and ministering to God's people.

In Romans 12:16, we find this "one another command": "*Be of the same mind toward one another;* do not be haughty in mind, but associate with the lowly. Do not be wise in your own estimation." Galatians 6:1 says, "Brethren, even if anyone is caught in any trespass, you who are spiritual, *restore such a one* in a spirit of gentleness; each one looking to yourself, so that you too will not be tempted."

These two verses get more specific on how we're to treat one another. We're commanded to live in harmony—not with fighting, arguing, or contention of any kind. Additionally, we're to be involved in holding each other accountable. If a brother or sister in Christ is caught in a pattern of sin, we're commanded to do what we can to restore that person so that they can function in ministry once again for Christ.

Galatians 6:2 continues, "*Bear one another's burdens,* and thereby fulfill the law of Christ." I Corinthians 12:25-26 teaches, "...but that the members *may have the same care for one another.* And if one member suffers, all the members suffer with it; if one member is honored, all the members rejoice with it." We learn in these verses that we're expected to rejoice, sorrow, be honored, and suffer with other believers. Other peoples' problems should be our problems as well, in the sense that we're to show compassion for them and assist them in any way possible.

Hebrews 3:13 commands, "*But encourage one another day after day*, as long as it is still called "Today," so that none of you will be hardened by the deceitfulness of sin." Hebrews 10:24 gives a similar command, "...and let us consider how to *stimulate one another to love and good deeds.*" In I Thessalonians 5:11, Paul also called us to a life of encouragement:

"*Therefore encourage one another and build up one another,* just as you also are doing." Additionally, I Thessalonians 4:18 says, "Therefore comfort one another with these words."

Though some people may seem to be naturally gifted at encouraging and uplifting other people, the Bible makes it clear that we're all to be encouragers. According to Scripture, encouragement is to be a regular part of our interaction with other people. This necessarily means that we must spend time with other people for the purpose of knowing their needs, their struggles, and how best they may be encouraged.

Ephesians 5:21 teaches, "*...and be subject to one another* in the fear of Christ." In Ephesians 5:30, Paul explained why we're to do this: "...because we're members of His body." Christians are a body; just as our physical body requires the constant presence of all its parts, so the church body is one entity in God's eyes. We all belong to each other, we're members of one another, and it is our responsibility to put our services and ministries at one another's disposal.

There are many other "one another commands" in Scripture that we must fulfill as followers of Christ and servants of each other. Paul wrote in Ephesians 4:1-2 that we're to "walk worthy of the calling with which [we] have been called, *with all humility and gentleness, with patience, showing tolerance for one another in love.*" In Colossians 3:16, Paul instructed, "Let the word of Christ richly dwell within you, *with all wisdom teaching and admonishing one another...*"

James 5:16 says, "T*herefore, confess your sins to one another*, and *pray for one another...*" James 5:9

admonishes, "*Do not complain, brethren, against one another...*" Romans 15:7 teaches, "Therefore, *accept one another,* just as Christ also accepted us to the glory of God." Romans 16:16 says, "*Greet one another with a holy kiss.*" And Ephesians 4:32 commands, "*Be kind to one another,* tender-hearted, *forgiving each other*, just as God in Christ also has forgiven you."

Implications of the "One Another Commands"

It's necessary to consider some important implications of these one another commands for believers and for the local church. First, we must consider the fact that the fifty-eight in Scripture are not suggestions; they're *commands*. Since sin is a transgression of any command of God, then not fulfilling any of these one-another commands is a sin. It's disobedience to God's law and contrary to His will for our lives.

Realizing that none of us can ever perfectly fulfill these commands, we must turn back to the cross. Every day we should be driven to our knees in confession of our failure and thankfulness for Christ's righteousness on our behalf. The more that we understand the depth and breadth of our "one-another responsibilities" to other believers, the more we will understand how sinful we are and how much we need to grow in godliness.

Second, we must consider the fact that all of these commands are in the present tense. This means that we're to be *constantly* doing these things. The lives of every believer should be characterized by the fulfillment of these commands toward other believers. We're to be constantly devoted to one another, praying for one another, honoring one another, greeting one another, and motivating one another to love and good works.

If this is true, then it also follows that we must be physically present with other people in order to do these things. A Christian who is not committed to a local church and rarely meets with the same group of believers cannot fulfill these commands. Not only that, but our contact with other people must be so regular that we're able to know their needs, their struggles, their joys, and their burdens. These "one another commands" require intimate, rather than casual, interpersonal relationships.

Third, we must consider the fact that most of these commands are contained in epistles that were written to *local* churches. In all of Paul's "one anothering" passages, he was instructing the members of a specific local church to act in these ways toward one another.

They did so because "one another commands" imply a need for selectivity. We cannot possibly fulfill these kinds of commands to every person in the world. We do not have the time or resources to do it, no matter how much we would like to. We have to be selective about the people with whom we're going to work in fulfilling these commands.

Obviously, for this reason, it's impossible for any believer to fulfill these biblical responsibilities to other believers without some kind of formal, regular, continuous relationship. That kind of relationship is provided by church membership. By formally identifying with a specific group of people, we're able to commit our time and resources to developing close relationships with those people. We're able to meet with those people on a regular basis and depend on their continued involvement in our lives.

Considering these things, some Christians might argue that involvement in a para-church organization is sufficient to fulfill these kinds of commands. Many believers have had the opportunity at some point in their lives to be involved in para-church organizations such as Christian schools, crisis pregnancy centers, mission boards, radio programs, and countless others. Personally, I've been involved in various para-church ministries at Christian counseling centers and at the Master's College.

While many of these Christian ministries are performing important services for Christ, it must be noted that they're not the church, as instituted by God. The church, as defined by the Word of God, is a group of Christians who dedicate themselves to meeting together for the regular preaching of the Word of God; who submit themselves to biblical eldership as described in I Timothy 3, I Thessalonians 5:12-13, and Hebrews 13:17; who regularly celebrate the ordinances of the church (baptism and the Lord's supper); and who practice and submit themselves to church discipline as laid out in Scripture (Matthew 18:15-17).

Taking Action

What does all this mean for us as believers? To me, it's clear that the Word of God indicates that the depth and breadth of our responsibilities to other believers cannot be fulfilled outside of the local church. For those who are currently members of a local church, I would encourage you to take time to think about your responsibilities as members of a church, to rejoice in them, but also to consider how better to fulfill them to other members of your local church.

For those who are not currently members of a local church, I would encourage you to think carefully about these things. I encourage you to search the Scriptures to see if these things are true (Acts 17:11). In the next two chapters, we will look at several more reasons why church membership is not an option, but a necessity for every believer. As you continue, pray that God will make these things clear to you and that your heart will be open to accepting His will for your life.

Application/Discussion Questions

1. Summarize and explain the reason for church membership mentioned in this chapter.

2. According to this chapter, why is it important for believers to know about the privileges and responsibilities of church membership?

3. How do the "one anothering commands" support the concept of formal church membership? What does this chapter say about why it is impossible to fulfill these commands of Scripture without church membership?

4. What are the specific implications of the "one anothering commands" of Scripture?

5. List some of the specific "one anothering commands" that are impossible to fulfill apart from a formal association with a local church.

When answering the question about the importance and necessity of church membership for Christians, a consideration of what the Bible says about the depth and breadth of our responsibility to elders and church leaders will lead us to only one conclusion. Thoughtful and serious consideration of Scripture makes it clear that we cannot fulfill our biblical responsibilities to elders and pastors as laid out in the Word of God without being a part of a local church.

What are these responsibilities? Hebrews 13:7 and 17 explain some of these responsibilities. Verse seven says, "Remember those who led you, who spoke the word of God to you; and considering the result of their conduct, imitate their faith." This command to "remember" our pastors and teachers and to imitate their faith implies that we know them well enough to know about their faith and the kind of lives that they lead.

We cannot imitate the faith of a radio preacher whom we do not know. We cannot know how real the faith of a pastor is if we only visit his church every other month or so. We can only obey this command in Hebrew 13 if we're meeting with a pastor regularly, listening to his words, and watching his actions. It is necessary for us to know a church leader's life and faith very well in order to determine if his faith is worthy of imitation.

In Hebrews 13:17 we're commanded by the Lord, "Obey your leaders and submit to them, for they keep watch over your souls as those who will give an account. Let them do this with joy and not with grief, for this would be unprofitable for you." Again, we see that specific leaders have been given specific responsibility for specific believers: they must watch over their souls and give an account for the believers over whom they're to watch. The believers whom they're to oversee and for whom they're to give an account are commanded in this passage to make the ministry of their church leaders a joy by the way that they live and relate to their leaders and other believers.

These commands carry with them tremendous implications for formal church membership. They imply that the church leaders have an identifiable group of people over whom they must watch and for whom they will give an account. They know who is in that group and who is not; who they're especially responsible for, and for whom they are not especially responsible. These commands imply that people have identified with and acknowledged specific people as their leaders; as the men whom they will obey and to whom they will submit. These verses are meaningless unless there is some kind of formal commitment and identification between the leaders and the people. Importantly, these verses call on people to obey and submit to "your" leaders, not just any and every Christian leader. This certainly implies a definitive and clarified relationship with a certain church and the leaders thereof.

Galatians 6:6 further describes our responsibility toward leaders of the local church. "The one who is taught the word is to share all good things with the one who teaches him." It's not possible for us to share all good things with every pastor or elder in the world. It's not commanded, either, because every pastor or elder in the world does not teach us. As believers, we're called to submit ourselves to the guidance of specific leaders and to show our appreciation for their ministry by blessing them with the things with which we have been blessed.

I Timothy 5:17 echoes this teaching: "The elders who rule well are to be considered worthy of double honor, especially those who work hard at preaching and teaching." In other words, those specific men whom we look to and from whom we receive spiritual instruction are to be shown great honor and given the support that they have earned. These church leaders have committed themselves to studying and teaching the Word of God and the Bible says that they're to receive their wages from those for whom they labor.

I Thessalonians 5:12-13 expands on this theme: "But we request of you, brethren that you appreciate those who diligently labor among you, and have charge over you in the Lord and give you instruction, and that you esteem them very highly in love because of their work. Live in peace with one another."

In his commentary on this same passage, Leon Morris said:

Paul wants pastors or elders to be loved and not thought of simply as the cold voice of authority. Love is the characteristic Christian attitude of man and this should be known within the church. Especially is this so in relationships like those between the rulers and the ruled, which in other groups of men are apt to be formal and distant. Christian love, agape, is not a matter of personal liking and it is in keeping with this that Paul expressly says that they're to esteem their rulers in love for their work's sake. It's not a matter of personalities. It's the good of the church that is the important thing.

The church cannot be expected to do its work effectively if their followers are not loyally supporting the leaders. It's a matter of fact that we're often slow to realize to this day that effective leadership in the church of Christ demands effective following. If we're continually critical of them that are set over us, small wonder if they're unable to perform the miracles that we demand of them. If we bear in mind the work's sake, we may be more inclined to esteem them very highly in love.[1]

In addition to what Leon Morris has said, I'm impressed by several words and phrases that clearly evidence the importance of formal church membership. Those words are "that labor among you," "that have charge over you" and "live in peace with one another." Again, the idea of identification and recognition and a formal relationship is suggested by all of these phrases. "Among you" implies leaders that are close by and with whom you have constant association. "Have charge over you" suggests the idea that there are specific, identifiable leaders who have recognized authority over you. No one can have charge over everyone in the world. In fact, no one can even have charge over all Christians in an area unless those people have formally acknowledged and identified with that leadership.

The text makes no sense unless there is a formal and recognized authority relationship between the people and their leaders. Live at peace with "one another" has no meaning unless the text is referring to people with whom you meet constantly. It's not hard to live at peace with someone you meet only occasionally or not at all. It's clear, then, that church membership is essential for every believer because our responsibilities to our elders and pastors require it.

Reason Number Three: Clarification

Still further, every Christian should be a member of a local church because membership has always been regarded as a biblical way of clarifying the difference between believers and unbelievers. Acts 2:41-47 says that on the day of Pentecost, three thousand people repented and believed on Christ. It also says that these people "were together" and "were added to the number" of those who believed. Their baptism and subsequent identification with the church was an outward sign of their new faith.

In the same way, Acts 5:14 records, "And all the more believers in the Lord, multitudes of men and women, were constantly added to their number." It is important to note that the early church had a *count* of the people who were part of their group; they knew who *was* part of that number and who *wasn't.* In I Corinthians 14:23, Paul said, "Therefore if the whole church assembles together..." This statement implies that there was some way of knowing who belonged to the church and who didn't belong, otherwise how could it be determined if the whole church was there or not? I believe that we may conclude from this and other passages that in New Testament times there was a formal membership roll in the local churches that served to distinguish believers from unbelievers.

Reason Number Four:
Orderliness In The Church Requires It

Another reason for insisting that every Christian should be a member of a local church relates to the whole matter of the orderliness of the church. In I Corinthians 14:40, Paul commanded that all things in the church "must be done properly and in an orderly manner." So, membership is necessary for the orderly administration of the church.

When we consider some of the things that the Scripture commands elders to do, such as watching over the souls of believers (Hebrews 13:17), it's clear that elders cannot watch over the souls of every believer in the world. Elders are responsible to watch over the souls who belong to the particular local church that they've been called to oversee.

In I Timothy 3:1-7, Paul laid out qualifications for church eldership. One of those qualifications was that a man must manage his own family well because, "if a man does not know how to manage his own household, how will he take care of the church of God?" I Timothy 5:17 says that elders are called to "rule well." If a man is to rule well and to manage the church as he does his family, then he must intimately know those he is supposed to rule over, as he would know his family.

Peter gave us another insight into the role of the elder in the church. In I Peter 5:1-2, the apostle Peter commanded elders to "shepherd the flock of God among you, exercising oversight…" One of the things that the Bible teaches us about shepherds is that they must know their sheep. The Lord Jesus, the True Shepherd, said, "…I know My own and My own know Me" (John 10:14).

Elders, as under-shepherds of the Lord Jesus Christ, are responsible to reflect and carry on the ministry of Christ among His people. In order to do this, they must know for whom they're responsible. It is impossible for an elder to exercise leadership over all believers; he must be able to focus his time and energy on a specific group of people who have formally committed themselves to him for oversight.

Eric Lane, in his book *Members One of Another*, put the idea this way:

> The church is likened in the Bible sometimes to a body, sometimes to a family or household, sometimes to a kingdom, sometimes to an army. For any of these organisms to function properly, order of some kind is required. The same applies to the church. The church is not just a loose connection of individuals; it is a closely-knit structure like a human body and has therefore to be rightly organized. For such ordering, it needs to know exactly who belongs to it. A family that sat down to its meal table or locked its doors at night, not knowing who was supposed to be there and who was not, would be an extremely

strange phenomenon. An army battalion that did not know whom to expect on parade would soon be in chaos. If the church is to be a true family and an effective fighting force, it needs to know exactly who belongs to it.[2]

Reason Number Five: Making It Public

Every believer ought to be a member of a local church because membership makes a person's commitment to Christ a public affair. In other words, when someone becomes a member of a local church it's a public statement to the rest of the world that they've identified themselves with Christ and His church. We may compare joining a church, in this sense, to what happens when two people commit themselves to one other in a wedding ceremony.

A wedding is a public declaration, as commanded by God, of a life-long commitment that has been made between two people. When two people get married, a marriage license is signed and added to the public record so that anyone who is interested can look it up. In the same way, when we commit ourselves to a local church, we're making a public declaration of our faith in Christ and our desire to be identified with a specific group of His people for the purpose of laboring together with them in the worship and service of Christ.

In New Testament times, church membership was considered to be a serious matter in that identification with a church meant that you had become a part of a group of people who were persecuted and demeaned; membership was not taken lightly and flippantly. People who became church members were committed to and serious about Jesus Christ. Thus, it became a way of making their commitment to Christ and His people public.

In the time of John Bunyan, it was a costly matter for people to become part of what was called a non-conformist church. Even today, in some places in the world where being a Christian may bring suffering and rejection, it takes real courage to formally join a church. At these times and in those places, church membership is a very public way of proclaiming a person's identification with Christ.

In the United States and other places in the world, church membership is not taken very seriously and, for some, it means almost nothing. For many, their church membership means nothing more than their membership at the local country club or some other organization. This is true mostly in churches that have ceased to be real churches in the biblical sense of the word. In churches that are faithful to God and His Word, that require a credible profession of faith, and that insist on doctrinal and moral purity, membership is still a wonderful way of publicly declaring one's faith in Christ.

When people know what a particular church stands for and who are members, those members' identification with that church becomes a way of publicly declaring their commitment to and identification with the Gospel, which that church preaches. Likewise, when a person refuses to formally join a church that preaches God's truth, his refusal becomes a negative testimony against that church and the Gospel it preaches.

Reason Number Six: Ministry Responsibilities

Every Christian should be a member of a local church because membership challenges church members to fulfill their biblical responsibilities to other members. Just as it's important for leaders of the church to know for whom they have primary responsibility, it is also important that the members of the church know who it is they're especially responsible to greet, to serve, to love, to encourage, and so on as the "one another commands" instruct.

Galatians 6:10 expresses this idea: "So then, while we have opportunity, let us do good to all people, and especially to those who are of the household of the faith." As limited human beings, it is not possible for us to do good to every person on the earth. We do not have the time or resources for such a task. Not only that, but the verb in Galatians 6:10 is in the present tense, indicating that doing good is to be our constant, ongoing ministry to other people. We immediately realize, however, that no one could constantly do good to everyone in the world.

It's clear from the end of this verse that we're not called to such an impossible task. As believers, we're called to a very possible task of serving a specific group of people within the local church, or "household of the faith." The local church provides the context in which each of us can develop relationships in which our continuous ministry opportunities occur. Through these relationships, we're able to find out the weaknesses, problems, disappointments, and needs of people. Through this constant exposure with the same people we're able to gather all the information that makes effective ministry relevant and possible. Through this regular fellowship with the same people we're able to do the good that Galatians 6:10 commands us to do. In this context we're able to fulfill the injunction of Hebrews 10:24. We're able to get to know one another in an in-depth manner so that we can effectively stimulate one another to love and good works.

Ministry is a responsibility for all of God's people. It's not God's will that ninety percent of the ministry should be carried on by ten percent of the people. It's God's will that every believer should be fully equipped to minister and be active in building up the body of Christ (Ephesians 4:12). It's God's will that "as each one has received a special gift," they should "employ it in serving one another, as good stewards of the manifold grace of God" (I Peter 4:10).

The context of the Ephesians and the I Peter passages make it clear that the inspired writers were primarily thinking about ministry that was performed as part of a local church and even within a local church. It's evident that Paul had the church in mind in that he was not writing his epistle to an indiscriminate group of individuals who happened to live somewhere in the area of Ephesus. No, he was writing to a church that had pastors/teachers who had the responsibility to get the saints ready to minister to each other and to build up the body of Christ through evangelism and edification. He was writing to people who had identified themselves with a church in which they could receive ministry and give ministry.

Similarly, the context of Peter's statement leads us to the same conclusion in that in chapter five he mentions "the elders among you." To them he presents the challenge to "shepherd the flock of God among you, exercising oversight" (I Peter 5:1-2). Questions: Where do elders function? Who were they to shepherd? Over whom should they exercise oversight? Answers: They function in a local church. They shepherd people who are part of the church they pastor. They exercise oversight over people who are part of the local church they shepherd. The words "among you," found twice in I Peter 5, are significant. These elders weren't primarily responsible to shepherd people who were not among them. To try to do so would be an impossibility. Time, lack of resources and lack of energy would have made this impossible. The people for whom they were primarily responsible are clearly delineated by the words "among you."

Keeping this in mind as we think of what I Peter 4:10 means, we must conclude that Peter was not talking to an amorphous group of people who floated around and functioned independently. Rather, he was writing to people who were part of a local church that had elders functioning as overseers and shepherds. He was writing to people who had identified with certain godly and gifted men for shepherding and oversight, and who were employing their special gifts in serving others within the local church.

To be sure, as indicated earlier, Christians are to do as much good as they can to as many people as they can, but being part of a local church helps them to be more specific about the where, what, and toward whom the main focus of their ministry should be directed. Trying to minister to everyone is a wonderful idea but, unfortunately, it's an impossible idea in that no human being has the resources, time, or energy to do it. Focus, selectivity, and concentration are essential parts of effective and productive ministry. The truth is that people who try to do everything and to minister to everyone will end up not really ministering effectively to anyone. Church membership helps a person to make important decisions about how and where to use the time, resources, and energy that he does have.

Every true church of Jesus Christ will be constantly encouraging its people to have a ministry mindset, and primarily ministry that is conducted in, through and for the church. We want Christians to consider themselves to be missionaries sent out by the church on behalf of Christ. In our church, we have tried to promote the excitement, privilege and responsibility of church ministry in many ways, two of them being in the form of a little handout page of questions entitled *Do You Want A Ministry?* and a list of ministry opportunities from *A Homework Manual For Biblical Living*. We've given these ministry idea lists to all our church members and sometimes have included them in our church bulletins to promote and invite people to ministries. I've included these items from the handouts to help you to understand ways in which membership and involvement in a church can provide unique ministry opportunities.

The ministry handout which is titled, *Do You Want A Ministry?*, includes the following questions:

1. What are three physical needs that I can meet in this church?
2. What are four spiritual needs that I can meet in this church?
3. Who can I pray for? What spiritual need can I pray for them about?
4. What needs are there in the church that I can pray for?
5. What can I do to help my children or other children understand the Gospel? What do my children need to learn about God and

how could I teach them?

6. With whom could I share the Gospel this week?

7. What person in my church can I call and encourage this week?

8. Who can I invite over for dinner for a meal for fellowship and spiritual enrichment?

9. Are there new visitors coming to my church to whom I can reach out and make them feel welcome?

10. Who can I write a note or letter to for spiritual encouragement this week?

11. What missionary that my church supports should I pray for and perhaps send a letter or gift to this week?

12. What are my spiritual gifts and how can I use them as part of the ministry of my church?

13. Have I asked the elders of my church what spiritual gifts they've observed in me and what ministry needs I could fulfill?

14. Have I asked other spiritually mature people what spiritual ministries they think I may be gifted for and in which I should be involved?

15. What special ministry needs is there in the church that I can fulfill?
    What training for ministry opportunities is going on in my church of which I could take advantage?

16. Who could I serve by giving a Christian book, booklet or tape of my pastor's sermons?

17. Who could I invite out to the services of the church? (Note: Research indicates that

eighty percent of the people in the United States have never been personally invited to a church sponsored event.)

18. What needs are there among people in my neighborhood or at my place of employment that I could meet as a representative of my church, and especially of Christ?

19. Are there some people I could serve by making contact with them, not to tell them about myself, but just to befriend them by being willing to listen to them?

20. How can I help others in my church to love God more? How can I help them to love others more? How can I help them to pursue good works more?

21. Am I an example or model for other believers in my speech, conduct, love, faith and purity?

In addition to these questions intended to be ministry catalysts, we also make our people aware of the different kinds of ministry opportunities that are available to them through the suggestions found in the book, *A Homework Manual For Biblical Living*.[3] That list includes fifty-one different kinds of service opportunities from which every person in the church could choose and be involved. I include a partial list of forty-one ministry suggestions to demonstrate that there are important ministries for every person in the church if they're willing to accept them. I do this to help you to understand how every Christian is needed, and can fulfill his responsibility to minister within the local church:

1. Involvement in visitation for the church;

2. Involvement in the tape ministry of the church;

3. Involvement in some aspect of youth or college age work;

4. Involvement in some aspect of the Sunday School ministry of the church;

5. Involvement in some aspect of the Bible study group ministry of the church;.

6. Involvement in some aspect of the counseling ministry of the church;

7. Involvement in some aspect of the mercy ministries of the church;

8. Involvement in the promotional, publicity efforts of the church (mailings, telephone calls, contacting radio stations for community bulletin board events, delivering posters, door to door delivery of brochures, making promotional telephone calls, etc.);

9. Involvement in fulfilling some aspect of the buildings and grounds necessities of the church;

10. Involvement in some aspect of the evangelistic outreach of the church;

11. Involvement in some aspect of promoting, developing and sustaining the missionary efforts and enthusiasm in the church;

13. Involvement in some aspect of the music ministry of the church;

13. Involvement in some aspect of the literature (bookroom) ministry of the church;

14. Involvement in some aspect of the library ministry of the church;

15. Involvement in some aspect of the tract ministry of the church;

16. Involvement in some aspect of the hospi-

tality ministries of the church;

17. Involvement in some aspect of the transportation ministry of the church (driving buses or vans, caring for the church vehicles, using your car for Christ);

17. Involvement in some aspect of the ushering ministry of the church;

19. Involvement in some aspect of the copying of materials ministry of the church;

20. Involvement in some aspect of producing of brochures and pamphlets for the church;

21. Involvement in some aspect of the secretarial needs of the church;

22. Involvement in some aspect of the fellowship meals, banquets, refreshment, or food ministry of the church;

23. Involvement in fulfilling some aspect of the carpentry, janitorial, maintenance, or repair needs of the church;

24. Involvement in some aspect of the publication ministry of the church;

25. Involvement in some aspect of supplying practical service to people in the church (mowing lawns, snow shoveling, leaf raking, meal preparation, etc.);

26. Involvement in child care for couples in the church when needed;

27. Involvement in some aspect of the nursery ministry of the church;

28. Involvement in some aspect of church beautification (flowers, painting, art work, crafts, etc.)

29. Involvement in some aspect of the Bible club or the Bible group ministries of the church;

30. Involvement in some aspect of the diaconal ministry of the church;
31. Involvement in some aspect of the financial endeavors of the church (keeping records, counting offerings, etc.);
32. Involvement in some aspect of the adult teaching ministries of the church;
33. Involvement in some aspect of providing leadership in some area of the church's ministry;
34. Involvement in some aspect of the discipling ministry of the church;
35. Involvement in some aspect of writing materials for the church;
36. Involvement in some aspect of doing research for the pastors of the church;
37. Involvement in some aspect of filing materials, arranging books and doing computer work for the pastors of the church;
38. Involvement in some aspect of the prayer chain ministry of the church;
39. Involvement in some aspect of the seminar ministry of the church;
40. Involvement in financially supporting the ministries of the church through sacrificial giving;
41. Involvement in using practical skills for the benefit of other needy church members (sewing, cooking, cleaning, nursing, financial guidance, car repair, etc.).

After reading this partial list of ministry needs in the church and thinking through the *Do You Want a Ministry?* questions, I think you can see that the opportunities and need for service within the local church are great; the gifts and abilities of every Christian are needed by the church. There's plenty for every Christian to do. Moreover, since no Christian can meet every need that's out there in the world, or even in his own community, he must make decisions as to where the main focus of his ministry should be.

Scripture, I'm convinced, indicates that the main loci of the ministry of every Christian (outside of his ministry to his family) should be in and for the local church to which he belongs. As previously mentioned, the Christian is to do good to all men. But, on balance, since he can't really do that for all men indiscriminately, he must make choices and church membership will help him to make the proper choice.

As mentioned in chapter one of this book, there are many today who are criticizing the ineffectiveness of churches, and even abandoning the church. Some are condoning or even encouraging people to give up on the church and turn elsewhere for their spiritual sustenance. Robert Saucy describes what has happened with some people this way:

> The reality of the church as the instrument of God and as His primary concern today is met with skepticism and incredulity....The resultant widespread weakness and uncertainty have caused many to turn aside, rejecting with castigation the church as the locus of God's activity. ...What is needed far more than denunciations is constructive criticism and renewed effort to seek God's ways in which one may be a part of the building process.[4]

I couldn't agree more. Saucy has said it well. It's easy to stand on the sidelines and find fault with the church's weaknesses, deficiencies and ineffectiveness; it's another thing to become involved in fixing the problem by becoming part of the solution. More dedication, more involvement, more prayer, more effort, more devotion, more service, and more humble cooperation and participation in the activities of the church are the appropriate responses to the situation. What are needed are more people who will formally commit themselves to the church and join with the leadership in more completely fulfilling God's purpose and intention for the church.

Reason Number Seven: Ministry Privileges

In addition to what we've just noted about the importance of church membership for the individual Christian in terms of his own ministry focus, church membership will also help the church to discern who should be given ministry responsibilities. To be sure, service for Christ is the responsibility of every believer, but serving Christ with our gifts is not only a responsibility; it's a privilege as well. In Ephesians 3:8, Paul wrote about his privilege to serve: "To me, the very least of all saints, this grace was given, to preach to the Gentiles the unfathomable riches of Christ."

The various responsibilities and offices of a local church—preaching, teaching, evangelism, administration, music, ushering, nursery care, etc.—should only be performed on a regular basis by people who have committed themselves in a formal way to that church. But, you may ask, why is that important? For one thing, it's important because when membership is a requirement for those who regularly serve in the church, it's a way of ensuring that those who do the ministry of the church are true believers who are wholly committed to the work that they undertake; it will also ensure that they will act in accordance with the church's philosophy of ministry and doctrinal convictions.

Not only that, those who refuse to become members may be indicating that they're not really in agreement with the church's philosophy of ministry or doctrinal convictions. Also, it may mean that they don't see the need for commitment, accountability and shepherding in their own lives. Perhaps, it's because of a lack of teaching—the kind of teaching we're giving in this book. If so, these people need to be taught. Or, even more serious, it may be that these people are unwilling to formally identify with a local church because they're unwilling to submit to its leaders, and to other believers as is required by Scripture. There may, of course, be other reasons why people resist becoming members of a church. But whatever the reason, this unwillingness to formally identify with a local church is an indication that they're not totally committed to that church and therefore should not be given regular, formal service opportunities. Regular, formal ministry opportunities are a privilege given to people who are willing to commit and submit without reservation to the total ministry of the church.

The Example Of Charles Spurgeon

Charles Spurgeon once described his intense desire to be a member of a local church in this way:

> I well remember how I joined the church after my conversion. I forced myself into it by tell-

ing the pastor, who was lax and slow, after I had
called four or five times and could not see him,
that I had done my duty, and if he did not see
me and interview me for church membership,
I would call a church meeting myself and tell
them I believed in Christ and ask them if they
would have me.[5]

Why was young Spurgeon, just sixteen years of
age at the time, banging on the door of the church
to get in? He was doing so for several reasons. First,
he knew that commitment to a local church and
obedience to its leaders was essential to his spiritual
growth. Second, he knew that he needed God-ordained and gifted elders to be over him in the Lord,
admonishing and instructing him (I Thessalonians
5:12-14) and keeping watching over his soul (Hebrew 13:17).

Third, he knew that God had commanded believers to respect the elders of the church, to obey them
in the Lord, to submit to them, and to esteem them
very highly for their work's sake. He knew that to do
anything less than this, since these were commands
of God, would be disobedience. Additionally, he
knew that everything God commands is good; and
that joining a church is one of those things. As Jesus
said, "…blessed are those who hear the word of God
and observe it" (Luke 11:28).

Though Spurgeon was just a new believer and a
relatively young man, he had a strong desire to obey
and serve His Lord and he knew that this required
a commitment to a local church. Likewise, if we're
truly believers, we will have that same desire to obey
and serve our Lord. If, however, we do not think that
a local church is worthy of joining, why should we
be considered worthy of serving in it? Just as Spur-

geon yearned for membership in order to use his gifts for the building of the church, so also should we desire to make a formal commitment in order to serve as God has commanded us.

Application/Discussion Questions

1. How does the Bible's teaching about the believer's responsibility to church leaders indicate the importance of church membership?

2. How does church membership clarify the difference between believers and unbelievers?

3. How does church membership help the church to function in an orderly way?

4. How does church membership make your profession of Christ a public matter?

5. What may a person's unwillingness to join a church indicate?

6. How does church membership help Christians fulfill their ministry responsibilities?

7. Why should ministering for Christ be considered a privilege?

8. What may a lack of desire to minister indicate about a person?

9. How does church membership help the church discern who should be given the privilege of formal ministries in the church?

10. Was there anything in this chapter that was unscriptural? Was there anything in this chapter with which you disagreed? Why?

1.   Leon Morris, *Commentary on 1 and 2 Thessalonians* (Eerdman's Publishing Co., 1991), p. 167

2.   Eric Lane, *Members of One Another* (London: Evangelical Press, 1968), p.19

3.   Wayne Mack, *A Homework Manual for Biblical Living* (Phillipsberg, N.J.: P&R Publishers, 1979), pp.161-163

4.   Robert Saucy, *The Church In God's Program* (Chicago: Moody Press, 1972), p.7

5.   Charles Spurgeon, *Charles Spurgeon at His Best, Compiled by Tom Carter* (Grand Rapids: Baker Books, 1988), pp. 33-34

Reason Number Eight: Accountability

Every Christian should be a member of a local church because its leaders and members can hold us accountable according to the process clearly outlined in Scripture. We don't naturally tend to think that the possibility of having our sin confronted or of being in an accountability relationship as being beneficial. In reality, we should welcome and even seek out spiritual accountability because it's a powerful tool that God uses to mold us into the image of Christ.

Confrontation is an act of love that benefits the one confronted. Psalm 141:5 says, "Let the righteous smite me in kindness and reprove me; it's oil upon the head; don't let my head refuse it…" Proverbs 9:8-9 teaches, "…reprove a wise man and he will love you. Give instruction to a wise man and he will be still wiser, teach a righteous man and he will increase his learning." Proverbs 12:1 adds, "Whoever loves discipline loves knowledge, but he who hates reproof is stupid."

According to the Word of God, the wise person welcomes accountability. If we're wise, we will want to be reproved and rebuked so that we can grow in our faith. While it's true that accountability and confrontation from other believers can take place even if we're not church members, the later stages of the process cannot. If, God forbid, we would persist in a sin despite the rebuke and encouragement of others, the full extent of God's plan for church discipline wouldn't be available to us for our benefit.

Considering this, refusing to join a local church is tantamount to saying that we're not interested in divine accountability in our lives. Eric Lane has said:

> Christians who refuse church membership are like a man and a woman who merely declare themselves married and move in without ever submitting to a legal ceremony. They have only thought of themselves and not of the society of which they're a part. Marriage is a public affair because, however private a matter individuals may think it to be, other members of the community have a right to know who belongs to whom and who is whose wife or husband. A society in which everyone behaved as this couple would be in sheer chaos. Moreover, their selfishness rebounds on their own head because, by refusing registration, they preclude themselves from certain benefits the state grants to married folk.[1]

I believe that one major reason that the church of Jesus Christ in the United States is very close to being in sheer chaos today is because so many people think of themselves as individuals rather than as part of the body of Christ. Christianity is not "every man for himself"; it's every man together for Christ.

Marriage is a good analogy of the formal commitment to the body of Christ. It's hard to imagine what a society would be like in which no one was accountable to anyone else and where everyone was free to express their selfishness without ever being called to account.

When people merely live together without formally committing to marriage, they may come and go as they please. Before I married my wife, Carol, I dated several other girls, but none of those girls made a formal commitment to me, nor I to them. When I reached a point when I did not want to continue the relationship anymore, I was free to walk away.

Once I was married to Carol, however, that freedom was gone. I was committed to continuing that relationship regardless of how I felt at any particular time. Problems had to be worked out, not walked away from. Though there were certainly times, especially in the beginning, when we may well have walked away from it, we stayed together and worked our problems out because we had made a public commitment to God and to each other. We had entered into an accountability relationship that we both needed then—and still need today.

More than that, a formal marriage commitment obligates us not only to stay together, but also to fulfill certain responsibilities within the marriage relationship. If I'm not fulfilling my responsibilities as a husband, my wife is obligated to call me to account for that. If I were to spend money foolishly or disappear without telling her where I was going, she would have the right to ask me what was going on.

In the same way, formal membership in a local church ushers us into an accountability relationship that we all desperately need. It's good for us to know that others are watching our lives and will confront us if we're not walking in godliness. It's for our benefit that we make a public commitment to be a part of a local body so that the other members of that body can know what they may expect of us. In an attempt to help people understand the privileges and benefits, responsibilities and commitments of church membership we have instituted the following procedure at Grace Fellowship Church of the Lehigh Valley:

1. They fill out an application form on which they answer several questions about themselves personally and about their Christian profession.

2. They're given a copy of our church constitution and asked to read it carefully. This document contains, among other things, information about our doctrinal position, our church covenant, details about membership (meaning, privileges, reasons for, responsibilities of), an explanation of church discipline, our form of church government, and a procedure for settling disputes.

3. They're expected to participate in a church membership class, which discusses the history of the church, the details of the church constitution; and gives them an opportunity to ask any questions they might want to ask.

4. They're given a copy of *Life in the Father's House* (a book about the church and church membership) and asked to read it before they join.

5. They meet with an elder (or elders) and give their personal testimony. They're also asked to explain why they want to join Grace Fellowship Church and whether they have any disagreements or concerns about the church. They're also given an opportunity to ask any questions they might have about anything regarding the church.

6. If they have a credible profession of faith and are in basic agreement with our doctrinal position, they're then formally received into church membership at a Sunday worship service. At this worship service, they're called to the front of the church meeting room where they're welcomed into the membership. The welcoming service includes a brief description of the meaning of and reasons for church membership, a time for them to publicly affirm their faith and commitment by answering several questions and a time for other members of the church to affirm their commitment to these people, to each other and to the church. The questions that are asked to the people joining at this time are:

1. Do you trust completely in the Lord Jesus Christ for the forgiveness of sins and the salvation of your souls?

2. Have you committed yourself to Jesus Christ as Lord of your life, and are you willing to obey Him in every area of your life?

3. Are you willing to make the Bible, not your own or anyone else's opinions, not your preferences or feelings, the standards by which you will govern your life?

4. In accordance with the teachings of Scrip-

ture, are you committed to loving other members of the church as you love yourself and will you attempt to fulfill with them the "one anothering commands" of Scripture?

5. Are you committed to preserving the unity of the Spirit in this church and to pursue the things that make for peace and build up other believers?

6. Will you faithfully study the Scriptures and seek to preserve purity in practice and beliefs in your own life and in the life of the church?

7. Are you willing to advance the cause of Christ through this church by your financial contributions, regular attendance and service?

8. Are you willing to faithfully pray for the ministry leaders, people and ministries of this church?

9. Are you willing to respect, support, cooperate with, obey and submit to the leadership of this church as they exercise their biblical responsibilities of shepherding the members of this church in accordance with Scripture?

Then, those who are already members of the church are asked to respond to the following questions:

1. Will you welcome these people into the membership of this church?

2. Will you love them and commit yourself to fulfilling the "one anothering commands" of Scripture with them?

3. Will you recommit yourself to fulfilling with them the biblical responsibilities of Christians to their local church?

This description of what happens when people become part of Grace Fellowship Church of the Lehigh Valley emphasizes several things: The importance of commitment and of making that commitment public; of our need for being accountable to and for one another; and, that formal membership in a local church is a means of providing the accountability that God says all of us need.

Every Christian, who knows the propensities of his own heart can sing with meaning the words of Robert Robinson's hymn, "O to grace how great a debtor, daily I'm constrained to be; let that grace now, like a fetter, bind my wandering heart to thee. Prone to wander, Lord, I feel it, prone to leave the God I love ..." Every Christian when he or she is thinking rightly knows that every day he or she is a debtor to God's grace because every day he sins and every day he is prone to wander. He knows that every day he needs the gracious help of God to overcome the wandering and abandoning propensities of his heart; that he constantly needs the help and restraint that God provides through deep relationships with godly people who will hold him accountable and fulfill the "one anothering commands" in his life.

Formal church membership where mutual commitments are made is a God-ordained means for keeping us from wandering into the highways and byways of sin. According to Scripture, Christians need others to regularly encourage and exhort them so that they will not fall away from the living God and be hardened by the deceitfulness of sin (Hebrews 3:12-13). Every Christian needs godly people who will get to know him so well that they can know when and how to motivate him unto love and good works (Hebrews 10:24-25).

Christians need someone to watch over their souls (Hebrews 13:17). How much plainer could God have made our need for the accountability that formal church membership provides than He did in these verses? In addition, Proverbs 18:1 says that the person who separates himself from other godly people is seeking his own desire (not God's desire) and quarreling against all sound wisdom (Proverbs 18:1). The plain, unvarnished truth is, that every one of us needs the accountability that comes from formal, regular, intimate relationships with other godly people. God knows and has told us clearly that every one of us needs the accountability that formal church membership provides.

Reason Number Nine:
Decisions About Time and Resources
Every believer ought to be a member of a local church because membership helps the church to make difficult decisions about the use of its time and resources. As we noted earlier, we do not have the time or resources to help everyone in need. Difficult decisions must be made about to whom the church will minister. Galatians 6:10 says, "So then, while we have opportunity, let us do good to all people, *and especially to those who are of the household of the faith.*" Along the same lines, I Timothy 5:8 instructs, "But if anyone does not provide for his own, and *especially for those of his household*, he has denied the faith and is worse than an unbeliever."

According to Scripture, our first responsibility is to our family. As members of a local church, we know exactly who is in our family and who is not. At Grace Fellowship Church, where I'm currently serving as one of the pastors, we're privileged to offer a counselor training and counseling service to the community. We have three men and a lady doing formal counseling right now, but it would take many more people to handle all the requests that we have for counseling.

As a result, it has become necessary for us to put a policy in place determining who will be counseled and who will not. Our policy states that people who are members of Grace Fellowship Church and those who attend regularly have top priority. We have committed ourselves to never turning anyone away who has identified with our church and looks on us as his or her pastors and teachers. We will make time for them and we're glad to do it.

This means, however, that sometimes we have had to tell others who are not members or regular attenders, that we're unable to counsel them. Though it breaks our hearts to do this, we simply cannot give our time and resources to all who are in need. We had to make a decision about whom we would counsel and who we could not, and Scripture makes it clear that we're obligated first to our family—our local church body.

In many ways, our policy is like the triage that hospital emergency rooms practice all the time. Just recently, I fell and hurt my ribs. When I arrived at the hospital, because I did not have blood flowing all over me, I sat in the waiting room for over seven hours before I saw a doctor. In the meantime, many other people came and went into the emergency room ahead of me. Why? Because they were in more desperate need of attention than I was. With them, it may have been a matter of life and death; with me it was matter of discomfort caused by fractured ribs. I was experiencing pain and suffering, but I wasn't in danger of bleeding to death. I had to realize that the hospital staff simply could not attend to everyone the minute they came in, so they took the most desperate cases first. In the same way, the ministries of the church cannot be extended to everyone who needs them. There are just too many needs, and too many needy people.

In the church, we have a God-given responsibility to take care of our brothers and sisters in Christ. For example, there are many people in the world with financial needs. I cannot help everyone that needs money. But, if my children experience financial need, it's my responsibility as their father to do what I can to help them. Likewise, if someone in our local church experiences financial need, it's our responsibility as fellow church members to do what we can to help them because they're part of our family in Christ. Formal church membership allows us to know exactly who is in our family—and who is not.

While we're talking about the issue of privileges, I want to introduce one other thought for people who attend a church, or more than one church, and enjoy some of the benefits of the church and yet will not make a formal commitment. It's a thought that actually comes from the writings of Donald Whitney. In his book *The Spiritual Disciplines within the Church*, Whitney says that the person who attends church and enjoys some of the benefits of the church, but refuses to join is like a spiritual hitchhiker who

"...wants a free ride. He assumes no responsibility for the money needed to buy the car, the gas to run it, or the cost of maintenance. He expects a comfortable ride and adequate safety. He assumes the driver has insurance covering him in case of an accident. He thinks little of asking the driver to take him to a certain place even though it may involve extra miles or inconvenience."[2]

This statement by Whitney is plain talk, but if you have been resisting formal church membership, it merits your consideration. Perhaps you've never thought about it this way, or don't want to think about it this way. Perhaps you think it's too harsh; but I encourage you to lay aside your defensiveness and pride and think realistically about whether there is any truth in his statement. If you do, you may have to admit he has a point. You may not be bothered by the fact that your failure to actually join the church you're attending prevents you from ministering in that church in an official ministry role. That may not be of any concern to you, but what about the thought that you are receiving the benefits of the churches ministries without making a commitment? Have you ever considered the question, what would happen to any church if every professing Christian did what I'm doing? What would happen to the church or the work of Christ in this world if, in the words of Whitney, every person became a "spiritual hitchhiker"? Please, I urge you to consider what a refusal to become a member means to the purposes of God in this world. Please, to change the metaphor a bit, decide to become a vibrant contributor, a participant, one of the players rather than sitting on the sidelines. Don't be content merely enjoying the privileges of the church, while not accepting the responsibility for actually doing what you can to make the church what it ought to be.

Reason Number Ten: Several Biblical Passages

Every Christian should be a member of a local church because of the teaching of several passages of Scripture that don't make sense, and cannot be obeyed, without formal church membership. For example, in I Corinthians 5:13, Paul said of a certain man who was living in sin and was unwilling to repent, "Remove the wicked man from among yourselves." A person cannot be removed from a group of which he is not already a part. It makes no sense to put someone out who is not even in!

In I Timothy 1:18-20 we find another passage that tells about people being put out of the church, or excommunicated. Paul wrote,

> This command I entrust to you, Timothy, my son, in accordance with the prophecies previously made concerning you, that by them you fight the good fight, keeping faith and a good conscience, which some have rejected and suffered shipwreck in regard to their faith. Among these are Hymenaeus and Alexander, whom I have handed over to Satan, so that they will be taught not to blaspheme.

Paul indicated in this passage that he had excommunicated these two men from the church. Notice also what he said that excommunication means; it means to be delivered over to Satan.

How is this so? It's so because being outside the church is being in Satan's domain. The Bible indicates that Satan is the "god of this world," whereas the church is the expression of God's kingdom on earth and is ruled by Christ, not Satan. Those who are in the world (i.e., outside of Christ) are in Satan's domain and under his authority. Those who are in the church are under Christ's authority (2 Corinthians 4:4; Ephesians 2:2; I John 5:19). Consequently, because Christ reigns supremely in the local church, it's a dangerous thing for a believer not to be identified with one. When we function on our own, outside the church, we're asking to be knocked around by Satan.

Matthew 18:15-17 is another example of a passage that is impossible to understand apart from church membership:

> If your brother sins, go and show him his fault in private; if he listens to you, you have won your brother. But if he does not listen to you, take one or two more with you, so that by the mouth of two or three witnesses every fact may be confirmed. If he refuses to listen to them, tell it to the church; and if he refuses to listen even to the church, let him be to you as a Gentile and a tax collector.

The authority of Jesus Christ is manifested through the church as long as the church is preaching and teaching the Word of God. All of its decisions and standards come from the Word of God. Therefore, anyone who refuses to submit to Christ must be treated as an unbeliever because that is how he is acting.

Though it may seem a completely unloving thing to put someone out of the fellowship of the church, Jesus commanded us to do this when someone refuses to repent of his or her sin, because He knows that we need accountability in our lives. In reality, since Jesus commanded it, it would be unloving not to do it. And, for this reason and for all the other reasons we have previously mentioned, it would be an unloving thing for us not to exhort and seek to persuade every believer to become formally identified with a true church of Jesus Christ.

Making a Commitment

Is church membership important? Should it be regarded as a vital part of every believer's life, or is it merely a matter of preference? The truths presented in this book can lead to only one conclusion: Church membership is not an incidental or optional matter for the Christian. Rather, it's an essential and important aspect of the Christian life. According to Scripture, being a part of a local church brings with it tremendous privileges, and serious responsibilities, that can be fulfilled in no other way.

In I Timothy 3:15, Paul called the church the "household of God, which is the church of the living God, the pillar and support of the truth." If we truly understand the meaning of these words, how can we think that membership in this body would be optional? I do not believe that there are any biblically justifiable reasons for not joining a church that preaches the Word of God faithfully and that functions in a God-ordained manner.

More than a hundred years ago, the great preacher Charles Spurgeon wrote the following regarding local church membership:

> I know there are some who say, "Well, I've given myself to the Lord, but I don't intend to give

myself to any church." I say, "Now why not?"
And they answer, "Because I can be just as good
a Christian without it." I say, "Are you quite
clear about that? You can be as good a Christian by disobedience to your Lord's commands
as by being obedient? There's a brick. What is
the brick made for? It's made to build a house.
It is of no use for the brick to tell you that it's
just as good a brick while it's kicking about on
the ground by itself, as it would be as part of
a house. Actually, it's a good-for-nothing brick.
So, you rolling stone Christians, I don't believe
that you're answering the purpose for which
Christ saved you. You're living contrary to the
life which Christ would have you live and you
are much to blame for the injury you do."[3]

Consider the points that Spurgeon made in this
statement. First, he said that there are Christians
who think they can be just as good by not joining
a local church as by joining. Second, he stated that
failure to join a local church was disobedience to
God's commands. Third, he believed that every
Christian is saved for the purpose of being in close
fellowship with other believers. By joining with
other believers in a committed relationship, as part
of a local church body, we fulfill Christ's purpose
for us: building each other up and evangelizing the
unsaved.

Fourth, he said that every professing Christian
who refused to join a local church was not fulfilling
the purpose for which Christ had redeemed him. In-
stead, they were insisting on having their own way,
apart from other believers. Lastly, he believed that
those who did not join a local church were blame-

worthy and doing injury to the cause of Christ by their disobedience.

It's important to emphasize once again that Spurgeon and other noted Christian leaders of the past did not believe church membership to be so important because they thought that it was the way of salvation. Church membership does not save anyone, and these men believed that wholeheartedly. They knew quite clearly that "there is no other name under heaven that has been given among men by which we must be saved" (Acts 4:12) and that salvation is by grace through faith in the Lord Jesus Christ alone (Acts 16:31; John 3:36; John 3:16, et al.).

That said, however, they also firmly believed that once a person became a Christian, it was necessary for that person to immediately become part of a local church, for their good, and for the good of the rest of the family of the faith. Though there are many today who attempt to diminish the importance of church membership, and even the importance of the church itself, we must listen carefully to their reasons for this position and consider whether or not the Word of God can support their position.

I strongly urge you, if you are a believer who is struggling with this matter, to examine the Scripture thoroughly for yourself. Think seriously about the reasons we have discussed regarding the importance of church membership, its privileges, and its responsibilities. I'm convinced that if you do this with a truly open heart, you will come to the conclusion that membership in the local church is not optional for believers.

If you are a believer and you are a member of a biblically sound church, I encourage you to think carefully about your privileges and responsibilities, and rededicate yourself to fulfilling the purpose for which you have been saved. We have been given a great task—to build the church of Christ—and we must not take it lightly.

When Moses addressed the Israelites in the book of Deuteronomy, he charged them with a number of responsibilities. After laying out their responsibilities to the Lord and to each other, Moses said, "And all the people shall say, 'Amen'" (Deuteronomy 27:15). Sixteen times Moses called on the people to make a public commitment to the covenant that was being set before them. When we join a church, we're making a similar commitment, and we should be absolutely serious about fulfilling that covenant.

I would be remiss if I did not address one last group of people before we close this study. Most likely, some of you who have read this material have come to the conclusion that you are, in fact, not saved at all. If this is the case, your main problem right now is not your lack of church membership; it's your lack of salvation. Your greatest need is to repent of your sins and believe on the Lord Jesus Christ.

Once you have come to Christ, I would then encourage you to seek out membership in a local church so that you may be fed from the Word, benefit from the counsel and leadership of the elders, and participate in the many ministries of the church.[4] As believers, we have been given a glorious task of building up the church of Christ. May God help you to search the Scriptures to find out if these things are true, to take these truths to heart, and to walk in obedience before Him in all things.

Application/Discussion Questions

1. What reasons were given in this chapter for believing that church membership is important?

2. Why do we need to be in an accountability relationship with other believers? How can accountability be a good thing for us? What are the benefits of being in an accountability relationship? What are the dangers of not being in an accountability relationship with other godly people?

3. What may be the reasons some people don't want to enter into an accountability relationship?

4. What point was the triage illustration making?

5. Given the fact that there are a multitude of ministry opportunities in the world, how do you make decisions about how you will use your time and resources in ministry?

6. Why do I Corinthians 5:13 and Matthew 18:17 make no sense if church membership is not important?

7. What were the most meaningful thoughts that were suggested to you through this chapter?

8. From your reading of this book, what decisions have you made in reference to church membership?

1. op. cit., p.19
2. Donald S. Moody, *Spiritual Disciplines Within The Church* (Chicago: Moody Press, 1996), pp. 52-53
3. *Spurgeon At His Best*, p.34
4. Please see my book, co-authored by David Swavely, *Life in the Fathers House: A Members Guide to the Local Church* (Phillipsberg: P&R Publishing, 1996), for a more in-depth discussion of topics covered in this book.

Author's Bio

Dr. Mack is a graduate of Wheaton College, the Philadelphia Seminary, and Westminster Theological Seminary. He has been married to his wife, Carol, since 1957. They have four adult children and thirteen grandchildren.